L I F E W A Y S

The Shoshone

R A Y M O N D   B I A L

Benchmark Books

MARSHALL CAVENDISH
NEW YORK

SERIES CONSULTANT: JOHN BIERHORST

ACKNOWLEDGMENTS

The Shoshone would not have been possible without the kind help of several organizations and individuals who have committed themselves to preserving the traditional ways of the Shoshone. I am especially indebted to the Shoshone-Bannock people for permission to photograph at the reservation at Fort Hall near Pocatello, Idaho. I also offer my appreciation to the Idaho Museum of Natural History at Idaho State University and the Bannock County Historical Museum for their assistance and permission to photograph from the collections. Additionally, I would like to thank the National Archives, the Library of Congress, and the Philbrook Museum of Art for furnishing a number of fine illustrations.

I would like to extend my appreciation to my editors Kate Nunn and Doug Sanders for their many insightful suggestions regarding *The Shoshone* and other titles in the *Lifeways* series. I would like to thank John Bierhorst for his careful review of the manuscript. As always, I offer my deepest affection to my wife, Linda, and our children, Anna, Sarah, and Luke, who accompanied me on our long journey through Idaho to make photographs and learn more about the Shoshone.

Benchmarks Books
Marshall Cavendish Corporation
99 White Plains Road, Tarrytown, New York 10591-9001
Text copyright © 2002 by Raymond Bial
Map copyright © 2002 by the Marshall Cavendish Corporation
Map by Rodica Prato

Library of Congress Cataloging-in-Publication Data
Bial, Raymond.
The Shoshone / by Raymond Bial.
p. cm. — (Lifeways)
Includes bibliographical references and index.
ISBN 0-7614-1211-5
1. Shoshoni Indians—History—Juvenile literature. 2. Shoshoni Indians—Social life and customs—Juvenile literature. [1. Shoshoni Indians. 2. Indians of North America.] I. Title.
E99.S4 B526 2001   978'.0049745—dc21   2001018496
Printed in Italy
6 5 4 3 2

Photo Research by Anne Burns Images

Cover Photos by Raymond Bial

The photographs in this book are used by permission and through the courtesy of: *Raymond Bial:* 6, 9, 10, 11, 16, 19, 22, 31, 42, 44, 53, 64, 65, 66, 67, 69, 72, 78, 93, 94, 95, 96, 97, 99, 102, 104, 105. *Western History Collections, University of Oklahoma Libraries:* 12, 25, 26, 27, 28, 29, 32, 45 ,48, 54, 61, 75, 87, 115; *Denver Public Library:* 59, 81, 82. *Corbis:* 84, 91; James L. Amos, 15; Bettmann, 41, 71. *Library of Congress:* 47. *Archive Photos:* Hulton Getty Collection, 51, 83. *The Granger Collection:* 88, 111. *Idaho State Historical Society:* 113.

This book is respectfully dedicated
to the Shoshone.

Contents

Author's Note

At the dawn of the twentieth century, Native Americans were thought to be a vanishing race. However, despite four hundred years of warfare, deprivation, and disease, American Indians have not gone away. Countless thousands have lost their lives, but over the course of this century the populations of native tribes have grown tremendously. Even as American Indians struggle to adapt to modern Western life, they have also kept the flame of their traditions alive—the language, religion, stories, and the everyday ways of life. An exhilarating renaissance in Native American culture is now sweeping the nation from coast to coast.

The Lifeways books depict the social and cultural life of the major nations, from the early history of native peoples in North America to their present-day struggles for survival and dignity. Historical and contemporary photographs of traditional subjects, as well as period illustrations, are blended throughout each book so that readers may gain a sense of family life in a tipi, a hogan, or a longhouse.

No single book can comprehensively portray the intricate and varied lifeways of an entire tribe, or nation. I only hope that young people will come away with a deeper appreciation for the rich tapestry of Indian culture—both then and now—and a keen desire to learn more about these first Americans.

1. Origins

Shoshone
life played itself
out in the varied terrain
of Idaho, including the
rolling hills of the Great Basin.

THE SHOSHONE (SHUH-SHO-NEE) HAVE TRADITIONALLY LIVED IN THE VAST region between the Sierra Nevada and the Rocky Mountains known as the Great Basin. Stretching from the desert country of eastern Oregon to northern Arizona and New Mexico, this territory encompasses nearly all of Nevada and half of Utah; most of western Colorado, parts of Idaho and Wyoming, and a portion of eastern California. The Shoshone shared these lands with other native peoples, notably the Bannock, Paiute, and Ute, with whom they intermarried and shared many customs. Like many tribes in the American West, the Shoshone told many stories about Coyote and Wolf. Both a trickster and a provider, Coyote was also the creator of the Shoshone people, as related in the following story from the Western Shoshone.

The Origin of People

One day Coyote was walking through the mountains when he met a pretty young woman. She was carrying a jug of water.

He approached her and said, "I am very thirsty. Please give me a drink of water."

She pointed to a place about a half mile away and told him to meet her there and she would give him a drink. Coyote did so and asked, "Is this the place?"

"No, it is farther," she told him.

She went ahead and when Coyote caught up with her, she again told him, "No, it is farther."

In one Shoshone origin story, Coyote was making his way through the distant mountains when he came upon a young woman.

In this way, she managed to trick him repeatedly until she reached her home.

The girl lived with her mother who asked, "Where did you get him?"

"He followed me," the girl answered in dismay.

Coyote began to drink some of the water.

"Stop that!" the young woman cried, repeatedly striking at him.

*S*hoshone women were well known for their skill in basketry. Here a mother and her daughter display their willow water bottles.

However, Coyote dodged each of the blows as he drank his fill. The young woman then told him to go into the lodge. Inside, Coyote noticed many bows and arrows in the quivers hanging on the walls. He suspected that these were the weapons of other warriors who had visited the mother and daughter and been killed by them.

Coyote was afraid of the beautiful young woman, but he was also very much attracted to her. That night the mother told him, "You go and make a bed outside."

Reluctantly, Coyote went to sleep on the ground outside the lodge. In the morning, the old woman said to him, "There are many arrows in the lodge. Take them and a bow. Hunt all day and kill many ducks."

Coyote did as she requested and returned with many ducks. The old woman plucked the birds and cooked them. They had a great feast that night. Thereafter, Coyote stayed with the women and went hunting every day. He was in love with the young woman, and they got married.

As the days passed, the old woman made a very large water jug. She carefully wove the basket and coated the inside with pitch so that it would hold water. When the basket was finished, the old woman told Coyote, "You must go home now. Carry this jug with you."

Coyote was very puzzled. Why must I now leave, Coyote wondered, and why does she want me to take this jug? But he knew that he should ask no questions.

The old woman added one last instruction, "Do not open the water jug during your journey. Do not open it anywhere. When you come to the middle of the country, you may then open the jug."

Overcome with curiosity, Coyote now wondered what could be inside the jug. However, instead of asking any questions, he simply did as he was told. Saying goodbye to his wife and her mother, he started his journey, carrying the jug, which was very heavy. What can be in this jug, he wondered. Why is it so heavy? Coyote remembered the old woman's warning not to open the jug, but he was so curious.

One little peek will not hurt, he told himself. With a rock, he hammered at the plug wedged into the neck of the jug. As soon as he pulled out the stopper, young men and women jumped out. They were all fine-looking people. As he continued on his journey, the inquisitive Coyote opened the jug again and again. Each time people sprang from the opening. Who are these people, he asked himself. As he came to the end of the journey, Coyote realized that the people were the children from his marriage with the young woman. And this is how the Shoshone and the other native people came to live in many small bands throughout the Great Basin.

THE ANCESTORS OF THE PEOPLE LIVING IN THE GREAT BASIN ARRIVED IN THE region some time between two thousand and one thousand years ago. Originally, they spoke a language called Numic (NUH-mik). In time the ancestral language developed into several closely related modern languages, including Northern Paiute, Ute, and Shoshone. These Numic languages, as they are called, belong to the Uto-Aztecan language family. It stretches from Central America to Oregon and includes not only the Numic group but Hopi and Aztec, among others.

The ancestors of the Shoshone made these stone drawings, known as pictographs, on the walls of Holden Canyon near LaBarge, Wyoming.

Over time, the people of the Great Basin split into three separate groups: the Northern Paiute, the Southern Paiute, and the Shoshone. The name *Shoshone* (also spelled Shoshoni) may derive from the native word *sonippeh*, meaning "high-growing grass," or possibly "valley dwellers," although the origin of the name is uncertain. The name may also come from a different native word, *shoshoko*, meaning "walkers," a reference to the Western Shoshone who did not have horses. The Shoshone refer to themselves as *niwi* (NUH-wuh) or *nimi* (NUH-muh), meaning "person," and *niwini*, meaning "people." Other tribes referred to them as "Snake," possibly because some Shoshone groups lived near the Snake River. The first English accounts from Meriwether Lewis and William Clark refer to the "Sosones or snake Indians."

The Shoshone gradually drifted into three groups: the Western Shoshone, the Northern Shoshone, and the Eastern Shoshone. The Shoshone bands came together for tribal councils, buffalo hunts, and

The vast territory of the Shoshone included parched deserts, shimmering mountains, and rugged hills blanketed with sage.

other major events. When they did so, the Shoshone did not consider themselves to be separate bands. A nomadic people, the Shoshone migrated to wherever game or edible plants could be found. The Northern Shoshone and the Eastern Shoshone became skilled horsemen and buffalo hunters.

The Western Shoshone roamed central and northern Nevada, western Idaho, and northwestern Utah, as well as the Panamint and Death Valleys in California. They were composed of several tribes, including the Gosiute (or Goshute), Cumumbah, Tosawi, and Koso (or Panamint). Because much of their territory was desert, life was especially challenging for the Western Shoshone. Struggling to find enough food and water for their own survival, they had little opportunity to develop a complex society. They lived in small bands, which came together about once a year. They traveled by foot and relied on dogs as beasts of burden, even after horses had been introduced to the Great Basin in the seventeenth century. There was simply not enough grass in their territory for the grazing of horses. The Western Shoshone survived primarily on seeds and plants. They occasionally ate a little meat obtained from hunting and fishing. Their religious ceremonies were based on the Round Dance, and they acquired supernatural power through dreams and visions.

The other Shoshone shared similar languages and some customs, but otherwise lived quite differently from the Western Shoshone. The Northern Shoshone lived in eastern Idaho, northern Utah, western Montana, and eastern Oregon. They were divided into bands: Western Band (including the Wararereeka), Mountain Band (including the Lemhi), Northwestern Band, and the Pohogwe Band (or Fort Hall Indians). The bands tended to gather in large villages for long periods of time. Over time, the eastern bands of Northern Shoshone began to rides horses and hunt buffalo like native peoples on the Great Plains. The Northern Shoshone also began to fish for salmon—a skill they learned from the Nez Perce who lived nearby in the northern Plateau country. Like the Nez Perce, the Northern Shoshone also gathered the bulbs of a lily known as camas. Dried and stored, camas was an essential source of food during the winter. The large villages of the Northern Shoshone were headed by strong chiefs who led hunting and fishing expeditions and made alliances with other tribes.

The Eastern (or Wind River) Shoshone made their home in western Wyoming. They later became known informally as Washakie's Band in honor of their greatest chief. Early in their history, the Eastern Shoshone had ventured to hunt on the Great Plains as far north as present-day Canada. Like the northern Plains Indians, they rode horses, hunted buffalo, and went to war in large, well-organized groups. Under the authority of a strong central leader, the Eastern Shoshone were the most strongly unified of all the Shoshone groups. During the winter, they scattered into small family groups and camped in valleys sheltered from the wind and snow. They remained in the valleys where there was enough grass for their small herds of horses until spring when they came together again. In the late autumn, under the leadership of a great chief, such as Washakie, they came together again and hunted buffalo.

*M*any Shoshone bands came to rely on horses for hunting buffalo and waging war, as well as moving from camp to camp.

After the Northern and Eastern Shoshone acquired horses in the late 1700s they gradually extended their buffalo hunting to the east. However, they increasingly came into conflict with the Plains tribes, notably the Blackfeet and the Arapaho. In 1782, a smallpox epidemic devastated the Shoshone and they were not able to withstand the assaults of their Plains rivals, especially after the Blackfeet acquired firearms. Later, the Northern and Eastern Shoshone were driven back to their original territory in the Great Basin by the Sioux and the Cheyenne who were themselves being pushed westward by settlers.

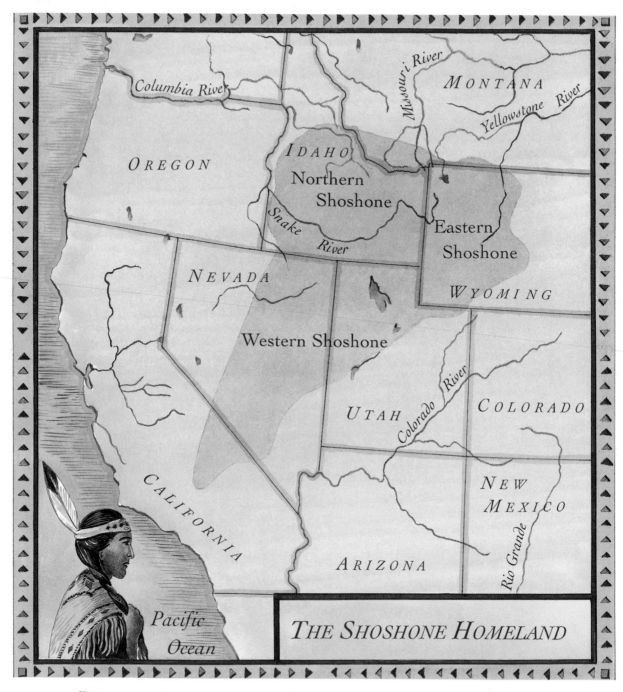

The traditional homeland of the Shoshone stretched on for thousands of square miles.

The Europeans and then the Americans became another source of pressure. The Shoshone first encountered people of European descent in the early 1800s when a young Shoshone woman named Sacajawea guided the Lewis and Clark expedition to her homeland. Over the next several decades, the Shoshone attempted to relate peacefully with trappers and traders. However, the settling of the Mormons in the Great Basin in 1847, the discovery of gold in California in 1849, and the opening of the Oregon Trail brought a seemingly endless flow of settlers through their homeland—and rapid, wrenching changes for the Shoshone. Although the Shoshone often allied with U.S. Army soldiers, serving as scouts and warriors, they at times also fought against these troops. By the late 1800s, the Shoshone were forced to abandon their homeland and move onto reservations.

The People and the Land

Hot, dry, and rugged, the Great Basin is one of the harshest areas in North America, yet the Shoshone adapted and learned to survive there. The Sierra Nevada and Cascade Mountain ranges block the moist air sweeping in from the Pacific Ocean. As the air rises over the mountains, the moisture is released as rain or snow on the western slopes. However, the rain shadow, the eastern side of the mountains and the rest of the Great Basin, receives very little precipitation. On some barren peaks there is not enough rain for any plants to grow, while other mountains support only scattered grasses and a few meager trees. In some places, however, there is often enough spring

Many of the mountains of the Great Basin receive little rain. Few plants can survive on their rocky slopes.

runoff to fill ponds and streams with ice-cold water. During their autumn dances, in the hope of receiving enough water, the Eastern Shoshone used to sing, "Send rain on the mountains! Send rain on the mountains!"

Much of this sandy, rock-strewn landscape alternates between mountains and valleys—with especially lofty peaks and broad valleys in the northern and eastern parts. Throughout the region, even on the flattest stretches of land, mountains are always seen poking up through the distant haze. The changes in elevation determine the climate on the mountain slopes. As one ascends the slopes, the air becomes markedly colder, and there is usually a little more rain and snow. On the valley floors, bristly cactus, succulents, and several kinds of yucca thrive in the dry soil.

There is great variety in the desert landscape. Warm deserts, such as the Mohave in southern Nevada and California, are dominated by creosote bushes. The cold deserts of the north are covered mostly with sagebrush and saltbush. Sagebrush and grasses also flourish on the lower slopes of mountains in the southern parts of the region. At higher elevations, there are forests of juniper and piñon and stands of scrub oak, ponderosa pine, aspen, spruce, and fir. In the north, the vegetation changes from sagebrush to juniper and piñon followed by another layer of sagebrush and grasses, then forests of conifers. In the far north, brush and grasses dominate the valleys, with forests of Douglas fir, ponderosa pine, spruce, and other large trees at the higher elevations. Above the timberline, a few small plants grow in the south, while lovely flowers cling to the craggy peaks in the northern reaches of Shoshone territory.

Along with the mountains and valleys there are canyons and plains. In the central and the southern parts of the Great Basin, the Colorado River has carved dramatic canyons with towering walls of layered rock. By contrast, in the north, there are plains of deep soil and lush grasses between the streams that flow into the Green and Snake Rivers. The region is also dotted with spring-fed marshes. On this moist, spongy ground of cattails and bulrushes, fish, frogs, and turtles flourish.

Otherwise the arid land is better suited for scaly lizards and slithery snakes, as well as rodents and birds that have adapted to the dry climate. In the true desert, the burrowing rodents include kangaroo rats and pocket mice. Horned larks, vesper sparrows, and western kingbirds glide through the air, while jackrabbits and kit foxes, symbols of the desert, venture from their underground burrows. In the sagebrush and piñon trees at the fringes of the desert are found other rodents—woodrats, ground squirrels—and cottontails.

Many of these hardy creatures were caught as food by the Western Shoshone. The Western Shoshone also hunted the pronghorn antelope and the buffalo that occasionally wandered into their territory, and in the winter they stalked the mule deer that descended the slopes in search of better grazing. In the mountains, bighorn sheep and elk grazed, and the Shoshone pursued them as well. Red squirrels, porcupine, marmots, and beavers were also often added to the cooking pot. The Shoshone shared the hunting grounds of the Great Basin with mountain lions, wolves, foxes, and hawks. Coyotes also wandered throughout the deserts and mountains, feeding on any small creature that came their way.

Salmon migrated seasonally to the rivers that laced the northern parts of the Great Basin. Trout and other fish abounded in the lakes and streams. Through each of the four seasons, Shoshone bands wandered through this territory as they hunted, fished, and gathered

Displaying their game after a hunt, these Western Shoshone families of Nevada did not move onto a reservation until 1940.

seeds and berries. Over the generations, they learned much about the plants and animals that provided them with food, clothing, shelter, tools, and medicine. They came to shrewdly understand the climate and territory in which they lived. Without this knowledge, the Shoshone would never have survived on the often harsh land where they had made their home.

2.Villages and Camps

Many Eastern
and Northern Shoshone
came to live in tipis. They
could be easily set up and
taken down when it was
time to move on.

DURING THE WINTER, WESTERN SHOSHONE FAMILIES CAME TOGETHER IN small villages named for a nearby landmark or a particular food that was gathered there. Although they lived together during this time, the families were so loosely united that none of these camps could be considered a band. Related by blood and marriage, the families shared customs. However, chiefs or headmen had little authority over the group other than to oversee hunting or gathering activities.

Northern Shoshone band leaders changed frequently, and people often moved from one group to another. Some bands, especially those that lived in the west, did not even have a chief. However, those in the east, such as the bands living around the Snake and Lemhi

Often, bands came together in a large camp for a buffalo hunt or a special event, such as the annual gathering for the Sun Dance.

A *group of men, including several Shoshone, took part in this Sun Dance hosted by the Shoshone at Fort Washakie in 1949.*

Rivers, often had to join together to embark on large-scale buffalo hunts and to defend against enemy attacks. The bands also united for councils and feasts, during which they were led by a principal chief and several other headmen. These positions were not hereditary and changed often. Band councils also arose to restrict the authority of chiefs. Groups of warriors formed soldier societies which may have also kept order during important gatherings such as buffalo hunts and dances.

Over the course of the eighteenth and nineteenth centuries, the Eastern Shoshone became the most organized of the three branches of the Shoshone—especially when the bands came together for the buffalo hunt in the spring and the Sun Dance in the summer. They also strongly united under a central leader when they battled the Blackfeet, Arapaho, and other tribes of the Great Plains. Holding the most vital position in the band, the chief had to have a range of exceptional abilities. He had to be wise and experienced—at least middle aged—and have the proven skills of a warrior and the training of a medicine man. The chief was responsible for major decisions, especially those regarding hunting, migration, and warfare. Along with his assistants, he had authority over two soldier societies as well. He also served as diplomat in any conflicts with other tribes. To signify his elevated status he lived in a tipi (TEE-pee) painted with designs and wore an elaborate headdress.

During the winter, the Eastern Shoshone separated into three to five bands and camped in the Wind River valley. Each band had its own chief and soldier societies to help maintain order. Families were not required to stay with their own band. They often joined other groups for the winter. Some even settled with other tribes, such as the Crow.

Dwellings

The Western Shoshone built cone-shaped huts, even in the winter. They sheathed these huts with sheets of bark. The Western Shoshone who lived in the mountains covered their huts with bark

The tipi continues to be a powerful symbol of the free and independent way of life of the Shoshone and other Plains Indians.

mats or brush. To protect themselves from the intense sun, the Western Shoshone built shades. To make a shade, they lashed together a framework of branches and covered it with brush. They sometimes placed brush in a circle to break the wind and provide a little shade. Some families, however, did not put up any kind of dwelling. When the weather got bad, they took shelter in a cave.

When the Northern and Eastern Shoshone made their home in the Great Basin, like many of the Western Shoshone, they lived in cone-shaped homes made of wooden poles covered with sagebrush,

A blending of the traditional and the modern—to the left of the tipi are a buggy and a car in this photograph taken in the 1910s.

grass, or woven willow branches. As bands gradually migrated eastward onto the Great Plains to hunt buffalo, they adopted tipis, which were better suited to a nomadic way of life. They covered their tipis with woven rushes and willows and eventually with buffalo hides, like the tipis of the Sioux, Cheyenne, and other Plains tribes.

Made of long, slender lodgepoles and stitched buffalo hides, a tipi could be easily set up, taken down, and hauled to the next camp. To put up a tipi, several women lashed three or four poles together and raised them, spreading out the bottom ends so the frame stood upright. To complete the tipi, they filled in the sides with ten or more smaller poles and wrapped a buffalo-hide cover around the cone-shaped structure.

Making a cover required hours of labor. Women first spread fresh buffalo hides on the ground and scraped away the fat and flesh with bone or antler blades. They next dried the hides in the sun and scraped off the coarse brown hair. After soaking the hides in water for several days, they rubbed them with a mixture of animal fat, brains, and liver to soften them. After rinsing the hides in water, they smoked them over a fire to give them a tan color. Several women then laid out several tanned hides and carefully stitched them together.

The covering was attached to a pole and raised and then wrapped around the frame. Held together with wooden pins, it had two wing-shaped flaps turned back at the top to form a vent, or smoke hole. The flaps could be closed to keep out the rain. The flap that covered the U-shaped doorway could also be closed. Men often decorated

*S*killed riders, the Shoshone still love horses like these pintos at the Fort Hall Reservation in Idaho.

over the back of their horse while women preferred a Spanish-style saddle with a high pommel, cantle, and stirrups. These saddles were often elaborately adorned with beadwork. Other riding gear included halters, bits, reins, lassoes, and rawhide whips.

The Shoshone—especially the Eastern Shoshone—became experts at raising and training horses as both riding mounts and pack animals. Male horses were gelded, or neutered, so they would be gentle. Men taught riding horses to move at several gaits. Some riding horses were specially trained for the dangerous work of pursuing buffalo. These buffalo horses had to respond to the rider's knees, so he had free use of his hands to shoot arrows or thrust a lance into his quarry. Packhorses, however, were taught only to walk and trot. The horse became a highly valued and essential resource on the long, dry stretches of the Great Basin and Plains.

3. Lifeways

The Shoshone have passed on handicrafts, such as exquisite beadwork, from one generation to the next.

Cycle of Life

The Shoshone observed many rites and customs regarding the key events in their lives—birth, coming-of-age, marriage, and death. Traditions varied among Shoshone groups living in different areas of the Great Basin, but they all valued the family upon which their survival depended.

Birth. When a woman was about to give birth, she retired to the menstrual lodge. During labor, she was assisted by an older woman who served as midwife. The mother remained there for up to thirty days. Her husband observed certain prohibitions during this time. For instance, he did not eat meat and he did not visit his wife or the baby for fear that he might bleed to death from the nose. A messenger told him of the birth, and later when the umbilical cord had fallen off, he was allowed to eat meat again.

Among the Western Shoshone, parents did not eat grease or meat after the birth of a baby. They were not allowed to touch their heads, considered the source of the strength and wisdom that was to be imparted to the infant. If they had to scratch their heads, they used a stick. A girl was especially welcomed because she would someday attract a mate who would help the family in its continual search for food.

Childhood. Shoshone parents rarely punished their children. Usually, a gentle scolding was all that was required to remind children that they were expected to be cooperative for the good of the

*S*hoshone women moved into special menstrual lodges, when they were having their periods or giving birth.

group. The Western Shoshone sometimes sang a song to warn their children that Wolf might snatch them if they misbehaved.

> *Furry Wolf,*
> *On his back he carries him away,*
> *Carries him away,*
> *Carries him away,*
> *Upon his tail he carries the child away.*

From an early age, boys and girls helped the women gather berries, seeds, and nuts. Children also raided birds' nests for eggs. In preparation for communal hunts, children helped to gather the brush used

The family unit was the nucleus of Shoshone life. Here a father carries his daughter on his back at a traditional gathering.

to build the corrals into which the jackrabbits and other small game would be driven. With bows and arrows, boys learned to hunt squirrels, which were gladly added to the cooking pot. With a pair of stones, girls ground pine nuts from piñon trees into a coarse meal.

Children also enjoyed a number of games that helped them learn the many skills they would need as adults. Northern and Eastern Shoshone children staged mock battles and buffalo hunts. In these imaginary hunts, one boy would bellow like a bull buffalo, and the others would pursue him. Children also played hoop-and-stick, a test of skill in which they guided a hoop over the uneven ground with a stick. Children shot arrows at targets and competed in footraces to develop the endurance they would need to survive the rigors of life in the Great Basin. Children also played a game similar to cat's cradle with a piece of string made from sagebrush bark. Using their imaginations, they always had plenty to do in the plains and desert around them.

Coming-of-Age. When a Western Shoshone girl had her first menstrual period, she was isolated in a separate hut and had to observe certain restrictions. She was not allowed to eat meat, for example, or carry firewood. The Western Shoshone required girls to remain in brush huts as a coming-of-age ritual. However, afterward women did not have to live apart whenever they had their period. Among the Northern Shoshone the opposite was true—every woman retired to the menstrual lodge when she had her period, but there was no puberty ceremony. Afterward a girl was given new clothes, and her body was painted to show that she had become a woman and was now ready to be married.

Young girls were prepared for the tough jobs of mother and wife. This included learning how to make clothing and often adorn it with elaborate patterns of beads.

Like the girls, boys also had to follow certain rules. A boy was not allowed to eat the first game he killed, so that he would learn a lesson in abstinence. As he approached adolescence, a Shoshone boy went on a vision quest. Leaving camp, he journeyed alone into the hills to seek a sign or message from the spirits. These spirits would help him to become a skilled hunter, so that he might support his family, and a great warrior, so that he might defend his people. The spirits not only gave him power but guided him for the rest of his life.

Marriage. Girls helped their mothers until they married, which usually occurred not long after puberty. A suitable husband had to be a good provider. Often, he was a somewhat older man who had

Shoshone men and women married and raised their children in close-knit families that formed the basis of their society.

already proven his skills as a hunter. The Shoshone did not have formal courtship and wedding ceremonies. Marriages happened in one of three ways: (1) A union could be arranged by the girl's parents. They chose a mate for her and usually offered the young man gifts to induce him to marry her. (2) A man could also simply stay with a young woman. He might live in her lodge for about a year or until their first child was born. Or, if she agreed, he might take her to his camp where they would begin to live together. (3) If a man saw a woman he liked, even if she was already married, he could capture her, often fighting her husband for her. In this case, the woman unfortunately had no say in the matter. However, she could later return to her family if she wished.

Death. The Northern Shoshone and the Eastern Shoshone wrapped their dead in blankets and placed the bodies in rock crevices where wild animals could not reach them. Mourners cut their hair and sometimes gashed their legs. They destroyed the dead person's horse, tipi, and other property in a sacrificial ritual. They believed that the soul of the departed journeyed to the land of Coyote or Wolf who were revered as great spirits among all the Shoshone.

The Western Shoshone buried their dead in caves or cremated the bodies, often burning the remains along with the home of the deceased. Mourners cut their hair, and spouses waited at least a year before they married again. It was believed that the ghosts of the dead could be very dangerous. Even dreaming about the deceased could bring misfortune. While in mourning, the Western Shoshone did not

*T*his cemetery on the Wind River Reservation in Wyoming is one way the Shoshone honor their dead.

eat grease or meat. They were also not supposed to wash during this time. After a year of mourning, a ceremony was held in which a leader symbolically washed away the mourners' grief. Objects that had not been buried with the body were also burned in a sacrificial fire.

Warfare

Warriors equipped themselves with shields, lances, war clubs, and bows and arrows. The Sioux referred to the Shoshone as the "Big Shields." Before they adopted horses, warriors fought behind large round shields that completely protected them. Made of buffalo hide, the shields were covered with painted buckskin. As they faced the enemy, the warriors stood close together so the shields touched, forming a wall. To further protect themselves, warriors put on sleeveless tunics made of six layers of antelope hide. With a mixture of sand and glue quilted between the layers, the armor could not be pierced by arrows. However,

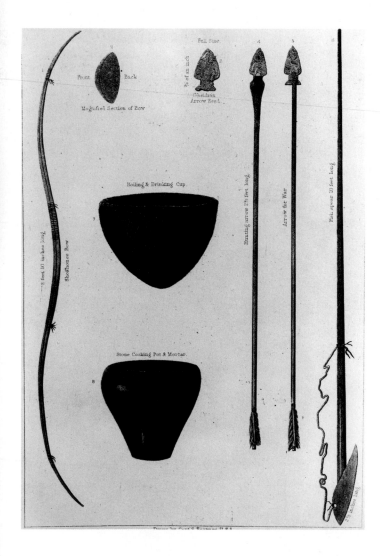

Both spears and bows and arrows served dual roles for the Shoshone. They were used as hunting as well as for warfare.

the tunics could not stop bullets, and as guns spread across the Plains, the Shoshone abandoned this form of armor.

The Eastern Shoshone were continually at war with other tribes from the beginning of the eighteenth century until they moved onto their reservation in 1868. They fought the Blackfeet and later the Arapaho, Sioux, Cheyenne, and Gros Ventre. During the late 1800s, they came to rely on the U.S. Army as their main ally. Warriors organized around two soldier societies: the Yellow Brows and the Logs. With up to 150 courageous young warriors, the Yellow Brows served as the vanguard, leading the way during migrations. They also kept order during buffalo hunts. When engaged in battle, they fought to the death. Made up of older men, the Logs guarded the rear of the band during marches. Members of both societies went to war in the spring and especially the fall. Warriors who proved themselves in battle were entitled to paint black and red finger marks on their tipis. Warriors were also entitled to blacken their faces in preparation for battle.

The Northern Shoshone traditionally fought the Blackfeet and the Nez Perce. Their weapons included bows made of cedar or the horns of elk or mountain sheep, along with poison-tipped arrows kept in otter-skin quivers. They chipped obsidian into sharp arrowheads and knife blades. In close fighting, they wielded stone war clubs. Antelope-skin armor and buffalo-skin shields offered some protection during battle. After acquiring horses, the Northern Shoshone adopted many of the war customs of the Plains Indians, such as taking scalps and "counting coup." Warriors counted coup by approaching an enemy close enough to actually touch him. To shoot an enemy from a distance did not require as much courage as riding or running up to him. Warriors also counted coup by stealing horses and undertaking other acts of bravery. The Shoshone also adopted the Scalp Dance from the Plains tribes. In the Scalp Dance warriors celebrated their victorious raids and battles.

The Western Shoshone historically fought the Utes. However, they had to devote so much time and energy to eking out a meager existence that they seldom went to war with other groups.

Hunting, Fishing, and Gathering

There, in a distant place, she sits in an arroyo,
winnowing the pine nuts.

By the red-rock-wooded place,
winnowing the pine nuts.

—Western Shoshone song

Like the tribes of the Great Plains, the Eastern and Northern Shoshone came to rely on the buffalo as their primary source of food. The Eastern Shoshone went on a buffalo hunt in the spring. This was followed in early summer by a Sun Dance, their most important annual ceremony. In the early autumn, they often joined the Bannock and the Flathead for a large communal hunt. In later years, they often traded hides and dried meat from these hunts for horses, pack animals, and European goods.

*S*trapped to a horse, the travois made the task of transporting goods across the Plains much easier.

Once a grazing herd had been located, young men rode out to it on horseback. Galloping alongside the beasts, these daring hunters shot arrows or thrust lances deep into the heaving chests of the buffalo. After the hunt, the women quickly butchered the carcasses where they lay scattered over the plains. Hunters had rights to the animals they had killed, but everyone who participated in the hunt received a share of the meat. The liver and other organs that quickly spoiled in the heat were cooked and eaten right away. The tongue, hump meat, and ribs, all of which were considered to be the choicest parts of the buffalo, were also cooked and eaten at the scene of the hunt.

Most of the fresh meat was loaded on travois and hauled back to camp. There, women sliced the meat into thin strips and hung them on wooden racks to dry in the sun. Sometimes, they built fires under the racks to keep flies away and quicken the drying time. Women pounded some of the dried meat, called jerky, into a fine meal and mixed it with berries to make pemmican. People sometimes ate pemmican as a snack, but most often men used it as energy food on long journeys. Most of the dried meat, however, was stored for the winter months ahead.

After the spring buffalo hunt, Eastern Shoshone women gathered fruits, berries, roots, and wild plants—notably camas, wild onions, and sunflower seeds—for the rest of the summer. Men caught fish—mostly cutthroat trout, Montana grayling, and Rocky Mountain whitefish—especially in the early spring when supplies of food were low. They made weirs, or traps, by placing rocks or brush across a

*M*en caught many kinds of fish in basket-style traps called weirs, which were placed in the currents of briskly flowing streams.

stream, leaving a narrow opening through which the fish were forced to swim. Sometimes, they placed a willow basket across the opening to scoop up the fish more easily. The fish were eaten fresh or dried in the sun or smoked over a low fire for later use.

Next to buffalo and fish, elk was the most important source of food for the Eastern Shoshone. The men either ran down entire herds or tracked single animals. They also hunted mule deer, antelope, moose, bear, and mountain sheep. Jackrabbits, beavers, and other small game, as well as ducks and other birds, also supplemented their diet. In the autumn, the Eastern Shoshone embarked on another hunt after the buffalo had fattened on summer grass. Through the long and lean winter months, they sustained themselves largely on dried buffalo meat.

Men grew up to become skilled hunters of game—*buffalo, elk, deer, and rabbits—which they killed with clubs as well as bows and arrows.*

Northern Shoshone men also not only pursued buffalo on horseback but hunted mountain sheep, deer, elk, pronghorn antelope, and other large game. Disguised in antelope skins, a hunter often crept up on an animal or, riding a horse, he ran down a fleet-footed antelope. People also caught fish, including trout, perch, suckers, and sturgeon, but mostly salmon, in the rivers that laced through their territory. Standing on platforms or wading into the water, men speared or netted the fish. They also built salmon weirs across streams. With sharpened, fire-hardened sticks, women dug prairie turnips, tobacco root, bitterroot, and especially yampa root and camas bulbs. The roots were either boiled or steamed for several days in pits dug in the ground. Hot rocks were placed in these earthen ovens along with the roots, then the pit was covered with soil. The women also gathered seeds and berries, especially chokecherries and serviceberries. Some Northern Shoshone also gathered pine nuts.

Throughout the spring, summer, and autumn, the Western Shoshone walked to the places they knew abounded with plant foods and animals. However, game was scarce in the desert and the Western Shoshone ate much less meat than the other tribes. Women picked greens in the spring and gathered many kinds of grasses, along with seeds, berries, pine nuts, and roots, through the summer and autumn. They made these seeds and roots into cakes. With digging sticks, they harvested wild turnips and other roots, which they then baked in pits beneath hot rocks until soft and brown. With beating sticks, women knocked seeds loose or they collected seed heads, which they tied into bunches. Small seeds and pine nuts were carried in baskets. In areas where piñon trees were abundant, the Shoshone depended on the pine nut harvest. The Panamint and Death Valley Shoshone also ate mesquite pods. They ground the pods between two stones and shaped the flour into cakes that were easily stored. In the desert country, people also sustained themselves on salvia seeds, cactus, agave, and gourds. Seeds were threshed and ground, then boiled, roasted, or stored for later use.

Although most of the Western Shoshone's food came from plants, men provided some meat for their families by hunting game, especially bighorn sheep and antelope and sometimes deer. Men either ambushed the bighorn sheep or stalked them. Antelope were driven into a V-shaped corral made of brush or stones where they were easily shot with arrows. Rabbits were another major source of meat. Often, the entire band joined in a communal hunt in which they drove jackrabbits into nets made of twisted grass twine. They trapped cottontails in deadfalls and snares. The Western Shoshone dug out burrowing rodents, especially pocket gophers and ground squirrels, with sticks. They also flooded or smoked the rodents out of their holes. The Western Shoshone occasionally caught fish in streams. They also hunted birds, including doves, quail, sage hens, and ducks. In some regions, people sustained themselves on grasshoppers, crickets, and insect larvae. During the winter, several families settled in camps near their caches of dried meat, pine nuts, seeds, and other foods.

Here's a modern recipe for the traditional favorite food of the buffalo-hunting Shoshone:

Buffalo Stew

Ingredients

2 lbs. buffalo meat cut
into 1-inch cubes

4 medium potatoes,
peeled and cut into 1-
inch cubes

6 carrots, peeled and
sliced

2 onions, chopped

2 stalks of celery, cut in 1-
inch pieces

1 16-oz. can stewed
tomatoes

2 6-oz. cans of tomato paste

2 tbs. vegetable oil

1 tsp. marjoram

1 tsp. thyme

2 cloves garlic, minced

1 bay leaf

2 tbs. Worcestershire sauce

1/4 tsp. pepper

1/2 tsp. salt

1/4 cup flour

about 2 1/2 cups water

Directions

Place the vegetable oil in large kettle or Dutch oven and brown meat (about 3 minutes). Add onions and saute until translucent. Add about 1/2 cup water (enough water to cover meat), tomato paste, and seasonings. Cover and cook one hour over very low heat, or until meat is tender. Add potatoes, carrots, celery, stewed tomatoes, and additional water to cover. Cover and cook 1/2 hour over very low heat or until vegetables are tender.

Remove meat and vegetables. Thoroughly mix 1/4 cup flour with 1 cup water. Add slowly to the hot broth, stirring continuously. Place meat and vegetables back in gravy and reheat. The stew is now ready to serve.

Clothing and Jewelry

Shoshone dress varied according to how close the bands lived to the Plains and its huge herds of buffalo. The Shoshone inhabiting the eastern and northern parts of the Great Basin made their clothes from buffalo hides and occasionally the skins of elk and other big game. They often fringed their shirts along the seams and decorated them with quillwork bands on the shoulders. Made of elk skin, the leggings often had fringes. The Eastern Shoshone decorated their clothing more elaborately than either the Northern or Western Shoshone, most often with buckskin fringes, quillwork, and, later, glass beads. They were especially fond of blue-gray beads.

During warm weather, Shoshone men usually wore only a breechcloth of animal skin, fur, or bark fiber. It was drawn between the legs and tied around the waist. As winter approached, men donned leggings and long shirts that hung to their thighs. Shirts were made from the hides of buffalo, deer, antelope, bighorn sheep, or occasionally elk. If skins were not available, women wove strips of sagebrush or juniper bark into leggings for the men.

During the summer, women wore a front apron made of animal skins or woven fibers, such as sagebrush or juniper bark. Sometimes, they also wore a back apron. As the weather became cool, they put on leggings similar to those worn by the men and long dresses made of animal skins or woven fibers. With sleeves reaching to the elbows and hems extending to the calves, the dresses were tied at the waist and decorated with feathers, hooves, bird claws, or elk teeth. Later, Shoshone women adorned their dresses with beads and patches of

This Shoshone woman has adorned herself with bead necklaces, a shell pendant, and a leather belt decorated with metalwork.

red cloth obtained through trade. In the nineteenth century, many women began to wear European-style dresses, but others—especially the Western Shoshone—continued to wear the traditional garments of the Great Basin until well into the twentieth century.

For much of the year men, women, and children went barefoot. During cold weather or times of travel, however, they put on moccasins made from deer, elk, or buffalo hide. Shoshone moccasins had rawhide soles and seams stitched along the outer edge. Moccasins for winter use were made from animal skins with the hair left on and facing inward. For greater warmth, these moccasins were also stuffed with fur or grass. Sometimes, people wore moccasins of woven sagebrush bark. In the late 1800s, women began to favor high-top moccasins decorated with beadwork. These moccasins were similar to the footwear of the other Plains tribes.

People often wore robes, usually made from rabbit skins. To make a robe, strips of rabbit fur were woven or whole pelts were sewn together. Sometimes, women made robes from the pelts of beaver, marmots, and other small animals. During the coldest weather, they bundled themselves in thick robes made from deer, antelope, or bighorn sheep hides, or they kept warm in thick buffalo robes. The Western Shoshone usually had only robes made from rabbit skins or woven sagebrush bark. By 1900, most people were wrapping themselves in Pendleton blankets instead of animal-skin robes. All of these thick, brightly colored blankets were manufactured in an Oregon mill not far from the Great Basin.

Traditionally, Western Shoshone women in California wore round basketry hats, while those living closer to the Basin favored a taller basketry hat. Other Western Shoshone women preferred helmetlike hats of woven sagebrush bark or willow. Men usually did not wear anything on their heads, but by the mid-nineteenth century many had adopted feathered warbonnets like those worn by men of the Plains tribes. With beaded headbands and a crown of eagle feathers, these ornate headdresses were worn on special occasions.

Both men and women sometimes wore belts made from strips of fur or leather. They also carried buckskin pouches and bags, which were often painted with geometric designs. Sometimes they wore

*W*earing traditional dress, this Shoshone man sports strands of bead necklaces and a fur-trimmed sash.

bands of fur or iron, called armlets, on their upper arms. Lewis and Clark noted that the Shoshone also wore collars made of twisted sweet grass decorated with porcupine quills, shells, or elk teeth.

Both men and women wore earrings and many necklaces. Beads made from small animal bones or teeth, especially elk teeth, were most favored in making jewelry. Sometimes, the claws of brown bears were strung with the beads. Both men and women pierced their ears from which they hung strings of beads or pieces of abalone shells. Lewis and Clark also noted that the Shoshone liked to wear metal jewelry, including pewter buttons, earrings of copper and brass, and bracelets of iron, tin, copper, and brass. Some men and women had tattoos on their faces, arms, and legs. Women were often tattooed on their chins. On special occasions, the Shoshone also painted their faces with designs of wavy lines and horseshoes, along with figures of snakes and bears.

As cloth became available, the Shoshone made dresses, shirts, and other clothing from calico, broadcloth, and other fabrics. By the early twentieth century, most people were wearing store-bought clothes. Women preferred long skirts or dresses, along with cotton scarves and fringed shawls. Many men began to wear tall black or white felt hats. As many of the old ways were being transformed or forgotten, the Shoshone no longer saw the need to dress in the same manner as their ancestors. However, by the early 1900s, a number of individuals had begun to revive the old styles. They refined their artistry, especially in creating elaborate beadwork designs on clothing. Among the best-known examples of distinctive artwork are soft-soled moccasins with floral beadwork in a pattern that has come to be known as the Shoshone Rose.

Handicrafts

The Shoshone produced handicrafts that helped them survive in an often harsh environment. They used materials from plants and animals to make tools, weapons, household utensils, and other everyday objects that were both practical and beautiful. The Eastern and Northern Shoshone depended primarily on the buffalo as a source of raw materials for their handicrafts. Like the Sioux and Cheyenne, the Shoshone began to record the history of their people on elk and buffalo hide paintings. Having become accomplished horsemen, they also came to make and value elaborately adorned saddles, halters, and whips.

In addition to the meat, the Shoshone made good use of virtually every part of the buffalo, including the hide, hooves, and bones. Stiff rawhide was stretched to cover drums and war shields. Rawhide strips could be braided into tough ropes, and sinew was used as sewing thread. Scraped to resemble white parchment, skins were folded and stitched together to make parfleches for belongings. The Shoshone frequently painted their parfleches and other rawhide goods with geometric designs, especially rectangles, triangles, and diamonds. They also decorated rawhide with beadwork in geometric patterns. The women tanned the tough hides into supple buckskin to make tipi covers, robes, blankets, clothing, and moccasins. Men fashioned tools—knives, scrapers, and needles—from the bones. Horns were softened and shaped into spoons, cups, and ladles. The hooves were made into rattles. Even the tail could be used as a flyswatter. For the Shoshone, a single buffalo provided the materials for most of their tools and household objects. They also burned dried buffalo chips, or manure, as a fuel for their fires.

The Western Shoshone wove useful objects from grasses, willows, and other plant materials. All the people of the Great Basin twisted plant fibers into nets for catching fish in rivers and rabbits in the brush. However, Shoshone women were best known for their basketry. They turned willow branches, sagebrush bark, and other fibers into dishes, trays, bowls, cups, and ladles, and many kinds of baskets used for gathering, carrying, winnowing, storing, and cooking. A basket was often sealed with a coating of pitch on the inside to make it watertight. Because water was often scarce, especially in the desert country where the Western Shoshone lived, it was essential to carefully store this vital resource.

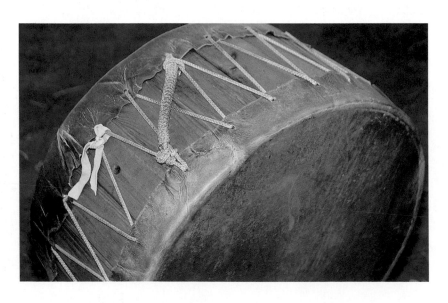

The Shoshone worked leather into many useful objects, including hand drums, which were beaten during songs and dances.

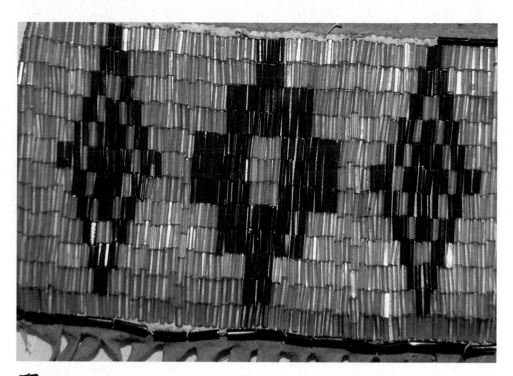

*B*old geometric patterns made out of quills or beads often decorated parfleches and other household goods.

The Shoshone also made use of many kinds of stones. They carved soapstone into pipe bowls and small dishes. They chipped other easily flaked stones—usually flint, obsidian, or slate—to make knife blades and points for arrows and spears, as well as scrapers, chisels, and other tools. With glue and sinew, they attached these sharp points onto feathered wooden shafts to make arrows. They often strengthened the wooden shafts of their bows by applying sinew onto the back. Arrows, along with a fire drill used for kindling fires while on a journey, were carried in an otter-skin quiver. Later, they traded for iron, which gradually replaced their stone weapons and tools.

4.Beliefs

The Shoshone often
journeyed to sacred
places to seek the help
of the good spirits that
dwelled there.

"The reason the Indian seems to worship the sun to some people is because the Indian believes the sun is a gift from God, our Father above, to enlighten the world and as the sun appears over the horizon they offer up a prayer in acceptance of our Father's gift."

—Dick Washakie, son of Washakie,
a Shoshone chief, in the late 1800s

Many Western Shoshone revered the sun, which they called Father, Appe. Some said he had created heaven and earth. Others believed that Coyote had created the world while some Northern Shoshone held that Wolf was the creator. The Northern Shoshone and Eastern Shoshone adopted the vision quest along with other beliefs and rituals of the Plains Indians. The Eastern Shoshone and Northern Shoshone sought the help of good spirits through dreams, visions, and journeys to sacred places. It was believed that these guardian spirits could heal illnesses, shield warriors from flying arrows, and bring misfortune to one's enemies. The spirits also told people how to use medicines to tap their own personal powers. People also refrained from eating certain foods and avoided various practices that were considered taboo.

The Shoshone believed that some people, places, objects, and activities had sacred powers—for good or evil. They feared ghosts and whirlwinds, both of which could bring misfortune. It was believed that sickness and death came from evil spirits or breaking a taboo. The Shoshone revered certain objects, such as eagle

Many Shoshone revered the sun—which they called Appe, or Father—as the creator of heaven and earth.

feathers and paints. They also honored certain activities, such as smoking wild tobacco, burning sacred grasses, and ritual sweating in lodges. In the sweat lodges they called to the spirits to help in healing themselves.

Most illnesses were treated by men able to effect cures with herbs, charms, and sweat baths. However, the Shoshone also had medicine men and women, who were specialists in healing. Among the Northern Shoshone, medicine men were especially skilled in the use of roots and herbs for treating injuries such as cuts and bruises. They also invoked charms and relied heavily on the sweat lodge in curing many ailments. Shoshone medicine men obtained their spiritual powers through visions during a fast on an isolated mountain peak or other sacred place. It was believed that Western Shoshone medicine men could also capture the souls of antelope so the fleet-footed animals would be easily guided into corrals.

Rites and Ceremonies

> Song Woman
> Sits beating the rhythm of her song.
> Song Woman
> Sits beating the rhythm of her song.
> There in a distant place
> Next to her cousin, the water,
> Beating the rhythm of her song,
> Beating the rhythm of her song.
> —Western Shoshone song

All three Shoshone tribes held seasonal ceremonies with much dancing and feasting. The Northern Shoshone held a special rite, the Round Dance, especially when the salmon returned in the spring,

*T*he Shoshone continued to express their deeply felt beliefs through ceremonies such as this dance held at Fort Washakie around 1892.

Ceremonies helped express the Shoshone's spiritual beliefs. But so did the natural world, which was an ever-present backdrop to their lives.

when seeds and nuts were harvested in the autumn, and during times of hardship. The Western Shoshone also held Round Dances during rainmaking and courtship rites, as well as during times of plenty. The Eastern Shoshone, in particular, held many celebrations, notably the Sun Dance and the *naraya*, or Shuffling Dance. Adopted from the Plains tribes around 1800, the Sun Dance involved fasting and thirsting. It was a time dedicated to visionary experiences and has been described as an occasion of sacred joy.

The Shuffling Dance was a kind of Round Dance in which the participants slowly moved in a circle, stepping with one foot, then dragging the other foot to meet it—to the accompaniment of song. The two main purposes of the Shuffling Dance were to prevent disease and to renew the earth so that plants would give abundant fruit.

Held over several days and nights during the summer, the all-important Sun Dance symbolized the strength and unity of the Shoshone as a people. Within a circle of twelve poles, men danced around a central pole topped with a buffalo head and an eagle. The men's chests were pierced with sharp sticks and tied to rawhide thongs which were attached to the sacred pole. Tied to the pole, the men danced for hours without water and endured intense pain. At the end of the dance, the men tore themselves free, the sticks and thongs ripping through their flesh. They took part in the Sun Dance to prove their courage and endurance but did not undergo the hardship for personal glory. Instead, they hoped that their sacrifice would bring cures and other benefits to their band.

Since about 1900, many Shoshone—especially the Eastern Shoshone—have been drawn to the Peyote religion. Originating among native peoples of Mexico and the American Southwest, this religion spread across the United States in the late nineteenth and early twentieth centuries. As they endured painful hardships, many Shoshone found meaning, direction, and hope in this religion. They believed that the use of peyote, a hallucinogenic obtained from a cactus plant, helped them to better relate with the supernatural world and renew their own spiritual powers.

Today, many Shoshone have converted to Christianity. However, others continue to devoutly practice their traditional beliefs, including participation in intertribal Sun Dances.

Games and Gambling

The Shoshone played a variety of games, ranging from juggling stones to jacks. Games were not only a form of entertainment but a means of achieving wealth through gambling and status within the group. The hand game was popular among the Shoshone and other native peoples in the Great Basin region. Sitting on their heels in two rows, two groups of people faced each other from opposite sides of a log. Any number of men could take part in this hotly contested game, but each side had one leader. The contestants used ten small bones as playing pieces and sticks as counters to keep score. One set of bones was plain and the other was marked with a black strip. The leader handed the bones to his players as they sang songs and beat the log with sticks. The players shuffled the pieces and hid them in

The Shoshone have long enjoyed many games, including the hand game being played by these men in Nevada.

their hands. The leader of the opposing players tried to guess who was holding the bones. If he guessed correctly, his side gained possession of the bones. If he was wrong, his side lost a counting stick. The side that had to give up all its counting sticks lost the game. People often became so carried away in a contest that they played the hand game all day and night, and often there was heavy betting on the outcome. The high stakes included horses, buffalo robes, and hides.

People of all ages, including men and women, also liked a dice game played with four sticks made from split willows painted red on their rounded sides. A scoreboard made of rawhide was placed in the center. People guessed and gambled on what number of each side would turn up with each throw of the sticks. The Shoshone also bet on footraces that were run over great distances, often by pairs of young men. During the summer months, when camped in the mountains, Eastern Shoshone bands often competed in games and races with the Bannock and other tribes.

Men also competed in a game called the ball race in which opposing teams kicked a stuffed leather ball across a goal line. Women often played shinny or double-ball shinny, a game similar to modern-day field hockey. Teams with five to ten people each met on a field about 75 yards long. Double-ball shinny was played with two buckskin balls that had been tied together. Each player had a stick and tried to toss or carry the balls over the opposing team's goal line. In shinny, players used a single buckskin ball about three inches in diameter and advanced it down the field with J-shaped sticks. A team had to score only once to win the game, but this was so difficult that it might take all afternoon to get the ball over the goal line.

People also liked to come together to listen to stories, especially during the long winter nights. Both entertaining and educational, these stories recounted the origin of people and the relationships among various animals. Here is one story from the Western Shoshone about how ingenious Coyote brought fire to the world.

The Theft of Fire

At one time all the birds and animals were like people and lived with them. But there was no fire in the land where they lived. One day, as Lizard was lying in the sun to keep warm, he noticed a strange object floating lightly down from the sky.

Rushing over, the people asked, "What is it?"

Coyote told them, "It is an ash from a fire in another country. Someone must fly high into the sky to find that place."

"I can go," said Hummingbird, and the little bird flew into the sky and looked in all four directions. After gazing toward the west for a long time, Hummingbird flew back to the people.

Everyone gathered around him. Coyote asked, "What did you see?"

Hummingbird replied, "There is a great body of water to the west. On its shore, many people are dancing around a great fire."

Coyote suggested, "We must go there and get that fire."

So, the people journeyed west. Coyote stationed some of the people at intervals along the way. As he and the other people approached the fire, Coyote disguised himself with a wig made from string. He then joined the people and danced. Luckily, they did not notice that he was a stranger. All through the night, Coyote tried to catch a little fire with his false hair as he danced with the people. Near morning, he at last caught the fire in his hair and ran away.

Even as they have come to embrace new ways, many Shoshone children continue to listen to the timeless stories of their ancestors.

Shocked that they had suddenly lost their fire, the dancers raced after Coyote.

Coyote hurried to the first man he had posted and gave the fire to him. This man ran to the next man. In this way, the fire was relayed along the route until it came to Jackrabbit, who placed the fire on his tail and sprinted away. Jackrabbit's tail was blackened by the fire—as it is to this day.

Rat waited in his house burrow on top of a rock high on a cliff. As Jackrabbit sped toward Rat, the pursuers caused hail to fall from the sky. Some of the hailstones struck Jackrabbit who squealed in pain as he scampered along the path. Hearing the cry, Rat scurried down the cliff. He took the fire from Jackrabbit just as the pursuers caught up. Eluding the pursuers, Rat scrambled to the entry to his house. He held the fire close, and it burned a red mark on his chest that he bears to this day.

Slipping into his burrow, Rat placed the fire in a large pile of brush. No one could ascend the cliff, so Rat and the fire were safely hidden in the burrow. But no one had fire now. Below the cliff, the people begged Rat, "Please give us some fire."

So, Rat flung the brush in all four directions and the people hurried to get a bit of fire. Finally, everyone had fire—and the brush still holds the fire. One can simply take a stick from the brush and use it as a drill for making fire. This is how Coyote and the other animals brought fire to the people.

5. Changing World

When the Shoshone moved onto reservations such as Fort Hall in Idaho, their traditional way of life was gravely altered.

SACAJAWEA WAS THE FIRST SHOSHONE TO MEET AND ASSIST THE LEWIS AND Clark expedition. For many years, the young woman had been held captive by the Hidatsa in what is now North Dakota. After being sold to a French-Canadian trader named Toussaint Charbonneau, she served as an invaluable guide and interpreter for the explorers. When Lewis and Clark came to the Great Basin in 1805, the Shoshone provided horses, supplies, and guides to help the explorers on their journey to the Pacific Ocean.

However, the way of life for the Shoshone was soon to change forever. "This state of tranquil happiness was interrupted by the unexpected arrival of two strangers. They were unlike any people hitherto seen, fairer than ourselves, and clothed with skins unknown to us," Warren Ferris, a fur trader, later recalled how the Shoshone had reacted to their encounter with Lewis and Clark. Ferris went on to recount, "Upon arriving at the strangers' encampment, they [the Shoshone] found, instead of an overwhelming force of their enemies, a few strangers like the two already with them, who treated them with great kindness, and gave them many things that had not existed before even in their dreams or imaginations." Yet the Shoshone were also "overwhelmed with fear, for we soon discovered that they were in possession of the identical thunder and lightning [firearms] that had proved in the hands of our foes so fatal to our happiness."

Following the historic meeting with Lewis and Clark, the Shoshone maintained friendly relations with trappers and traders through the early 1800s. Some bands went to war against the intruders while others sought to live peacefully with them. The

*T*he trapper and trader Toussaint Charbonneau, standing to the right, helped guide part of Lewis and Clark's expedition. By his side, his wife, Sacajawea, explains to the fast-approaching Chinook Indians the purpose of their intrusion.

Courageous Shoshone warriors fought a losing war for their freedom and their homeland, which were ultimately taken forcibly from them.

Northern Shoshone fought both settlers and soldiers whom they viewed as invaders in their territory. Shoshone resistance to western expansion into and through their territory lasted just four years (1861–1865). While Union soldiers were occupied fighting the Civil War, Native Americans of the Great Basin, including the Shoshone, attacked wagon trains, Pony Express riders, and crews stringing telegraph lines.

To protect the travel routes, Patrick E. Connor formed the 3rd California Infantry of volunteers. In 1862, these troops established Fort Douglas in the foothills of the Wasatch Mountains, a range of the Rocky Mountains north of Salt Lake City. From this base, they patrolled areas of Nevada, Idaho, and Wyoming. In January 1863, Connor led his three hundred volunteers north toward the village of Chief Bear Hunter whose Northern Shoshone had been attacking travelers through the region. The volunteers trudged 140 miles through the fierce cold and deep snow to reach the village.

Bear Hunter's people had put up barricades of rocks and soil to better defend the village, which was situated in a ravine. However, the troops outflanked the Shoshone warriors and, on the morning of January 29, devastated them with torrents of gunfire. In just four hours, as many as 250 Shoshone, including Bear Hunter, were slaughtered. Mormons who went to the site recalled "the dead were eight feet deep in one place." The volunteers destroyed more than seventy lodges and captured 175 horses, while only fourteen were killed and forty-nine were wounded among their own forces.

Confronting the overwhelming military power of the soldiers, the Shoshone realized that they would have to make peace.

In 1863, the Shoshone reluctantly signed the Treaty of Fort Bridger in which they agreed to sell much of their land. However, the payments were apparently never made. By 1865, hostilities in the Great Basin had ceased, and the U.S. government had begun to force the Native Americans living there, including all the Shoshone, onto reservations. The Shoshone opposed relocation. The Northern Shoshone were forced nonetheless to move onto several reservations, including the Fort Hall Reservation in southeastern Idaho and the Duck Valley Reservation along the Nevada–Idaho border. The Western Shoshone also resisted removal, but in compliance with the treaty signed in 1863, they eventually abandoned their traditional way of life and moved onto reservations. One band of mixed Shoshone and Bannock people known as the Mountain Sheep Eaters fought against removal until as late as 1878 when they too eventually relented and relocated.

Throughout the 1870s, the Eastern Shoshone under Washakie allied with the U.S. Army in wars against the Sioux, Cheyenne, Arapaho, and Ute, mainly by serving as scouts in military campaigns. During the Sioux War of 1876, Washakie led a band of two hundred Shoshone, Bannock, and Ute warriors across the Rockies to fight alongside army troops under General George Crook. Although Washakie arrived too late to take part in the battle, he and his warriors helped pursue Crazy Horse and his Sioux followers.

The Shoshone were pressured to abandon their traditional ways. These children are preparing to leave the Duck Valley Reservation to attend school in 1901.

For this portrait, Chief Washakie posed in his long headdress fashioned from eagle feathers with his peace pipe in hand.

Washakie and his people had been granted a large reservation in the Wind River valley of Wyoming. However, over the years, the size of the reservation was drastically reduced as later agreements were forced upon the Eastern Shoshone. In 1878, the Shoshone were compromised further when the Arapaho, their traditional enemies, were moved to Wind River to share the reservation with them. Washakie nonetheless advised that they continue friendly relations with the government. That year President Ulysses S. Grant presented him with a saddle adorned with silver in recognition of his help over the years. In 1883, while on a fishing trip to Yellowstone National Park, President Chester Arthur visited Washakie. In 1897, after his son died in a senseless brawl, the great chief converted to Christianity. Three years later, he died at Flathead Village in the Bitterroot Valley of Montana and was buried in the Fort Washakie cemetery with full military honors. The inscription on his tombstone reads: "Always loyal to the Government and his white brothers."

Throughout his life, Washakie was famed not only for his skill and courage in battle, but for his friendship with pioneers and his loyalty to the U.S. government. In the 1850s, when wagon trains had passed through Shoshone territory that bordered the Oregon Trail, Washakie and his people had helped the overland travelers to ford streams and recover their cattle that had strayed away. He had ably served as a scout for the U.S. Army and a trusted ally during the wars with the Plains Indians. However, as he approached the end of his life, Washakie believed that he and his people had ultimately been betrayed by those whom they had so generously assisted. He voiced his outrage in the following statement:

The white man, who possesses this whole vast country from sea to sea, who roams over it at pleasure and lives where he likes, cannot know the cramp we feel in this little spot, with the underlying remembrance of the fact, which you know as well as we, that every foot of what you proudly call America not very long ago belonged to the red man. The Great Spirit gave it to us. There was room for all His many tribes, and all were happy in their freedom.

The white man's government promised that if we, the Shoshones, would be content with the little patch allowed us, it would keep us well supplied with everything necessary to comfortable living, and would see that no white man should cross our borders for our game or anything that is ours. But it has not kept its word! The white man kills our game, captures our furs, and sometimes feeds his herds upon our meadows. And your great and mighty government—oh sir, I hesitate, for I cannot tell the half! It does not protect our rights. It leaves us without the promised seed, without tools for cultivating the land, without implements for harvesting our crops, without breeding animals better than ours, without the food we still lack, after all we can do, without the many comforts we cannot produce, without the schools we so much need for our children.

I say again, the government does not keep its word!

This illustration of warriors on horseback depicts the heroic battles on Chief Washakie as he struggled to save his homeland.

Shoshone Language

Shoshone belongs to a Central Numic group of the Uto-Aztecan language family. Central Numic includes three languages: Panamint, Shoshone, and Comanche. Within Shoshone there are three regional variations, or dialects, called Northern, Eastern, and Western. Since the differences are slight, any one of these dialects can be understood by all Shoshone people.

The following examples are based primarily on *Newe Natekwinappeh: Shoshoni Stories and Dictionary* compiled by Wick R. Miller. Shoshone is a complicated language, but the following key and examples should be helpful for the basic pronunciation of words.

Vowels are generally pronounced as follows:

a	as in father
e	as in pan
i	as in tin
o	as in go
u	as in put

E is unlike *e* in English, but similar to *a* in pan.

In some cases, vowels are written twice as in *aa*. These vowels are stressed somewhat more than single vowels. When vowels occur together, as in *ia* and *ea*, they usually have the same sounds as when spoken separately. However, *ai* is pronounced either as the *i* in bite or the *e* in bet. In the latter case, the *ai* is underlined.

The consonants are generally pronounced as in English, except for the glottal stop, a catch in the throat, as in the slight pause between uh oh! A glottal stop is indicated by a '.

Here are some everyday words used by the Shoshone:

Expressions

hello	pehnaho
no	kai
okay	maikkuh, tsumaikku
yes	haa

People

aunt	paha, tokka
boy	tuine, natuipittsi, piia
brother (older)	papi
brother (younger)	tami
father	appe
friend	haintseh, te'i
girl	nai-pin
man	tainkwa, tsuku, tuittsi
mother	pia, pii
sister (older)	patsi
sister (younger)	nammi
uncle	ata, hai, tsukuhnaa
woman	wa'ippe

Body Parts

arm	peta
chest	nenkappeh, yenka-ppeh

ear	nainkih
elbow	kii-ppeh
eye	puih
face	kopai
finger	maseki
foot	nampai
hand	mo'o
head	pam-pin
heart	pihyen
knee	tanka-ppeh
leg	oon
mouth	tempai
nose	mu-pin, muitsun
shoulder	tsoa-ppeh
toe	taseki

Natural World

cloud	pakena-ppeh
earth	soko-ppeh
moon	mea
mountain	toya-pin
sky	tukum-pin
snow	takka
sun	tapai

tree	soho-pin
valley	yakun
water	paa

Animals

antelope	kwahaten, wantsi
bear	weeta, akoai
bird	kwinaa, huittsuu
buffalo	kuittsun
coyote	itsa-ppe
deer	teheyan
dog	satii
duck	peyan
eagle	kwinaa
egg	noyo
elk	pateheyan
fish	painkwi, akai
frog	waako
horse	punku
rabbit, cottontail	tapun
rabbit, jack	kammu
rattlesnake	tokoa
salmon	akai
sheep, mountain	tukku

6. New Ways

Today, children enjoy coming to powwows, such as the Shoshone-Bannock Indian Festival held annually at the Fort Hall Reservation in Idaho.

Having just been selected queen of the Shoshone-Bannock Indian Festival, this young woman beams to the crowd.

education, health, and social services. Tribal leaders also manage agriculture, business enterprises, tourism, and other revenue-generating operations for the reservation.

While adapting to a modern way of life, the Shoshone have also worked to preserve their language and traditions throughout the Great Basin. Like Coyote, they continue to be skillful and clever survivors. Wherever they make their home, the Shoshone are both embracing technological innovations and striving to maintain their artistic traditions, language, and heritage for themselves and future generations.

More About

the Shoshone

NATIVE AMERICAN CRAFTS

Time Line

before 1000 The ancestors of the Shoshone make their way into the Great Basin.

about 1700 The Shoshone and other Native Americans east of the Rocky Mountains acquire horses.

1782 Eastern Shoshone are devastated by a smallpox epidemic and attacks by the Blackfeet.

about 1788 Sacajawea is born in northern Shoshone territory in what is now Idaho.

1803 President Thomas Jefferson acquires from France for $15 million a vast tract of land west of the Mississippi River known as the Louisiana Purchase.

1804–1805 The Lewis and Clark expedition explores the American West. The group eventually reaches the Pacific Ocean with the help of the Shoshone and Sacajawea as a guide.

1847 Mormons settle in Shoshone territory in the Salt Lake Valley of Utah.

1848 In the Treaty of Guadalupe Hidalgo, Mexico cedes a large tract of land, including Shoshone territory, to the United States. Gold is discovered in California.

1859 Settlers pour into Nevada when gold and silver mines open at the Comstock Lode.

1863 The Shoshone are defeated in the Battle of Bear River, also known as the Bear River Massacre or the Bannock Wars.

1869 President Ulysses S. Grant introduces policies to extinguish Native American traditions and religions.

1900 Chief Washakie dies.

1934 The Indian Reorganization Act grants Native Americans greater control of their tribal affairs.

1972 The Indian Self-Determination Act grants tribes more control over local laws and greater involvement in government policy.

1982 The Western Shoshone are recognized as a tribe by the federal government.

1984 The Western Shoshone National Council is formed to handle tribal land claims.

1988 The Wind River Shoshone form a task force to study living conditions on their reservation.

1991 To stimulate economic growth, the Northern Shoshone open gambling operations on their reservation.

Notable People

Bear Hunter (Wirasuap, Bear Spirit) (died 1863) lived in a village along the Bear River that flows into the Great Salt Lake in Utah. During the early 1860s, Native Americans in the Great Basin, including Bear Hunter, often made raids against the miners and Mormons. They also attacked wagon trains and stagecoaches on the Central Overland Route to California, as well as Pony Express riders and crews putting up telegraph lines.

Because U.S. troops were involved with the Civil War, they were not available to protect settlers and travelers in the West. To keep the routes open, the 3rd California Infantry of volunteers was organized under Patrick E. Connor. In 1862, these troops established Fort Douglas in the foothills of the Wasatch Mountains, a range of the Rocky Mountains overlooking Salt Lake City. From this base, they patrolled areas of Nevada, Idaho, and Wyoming. In January 1863, Connor led a force of three hundred troops northward toward Bear Hunter's village. The men trudged 140 miles through bitter cold and deep snow to devastate the village with gunfire. In the fighting that lasted four hours, as many as 250 Shoshone, including Bear Hunter, were killed. The Shoshone were later forced to sign a treaty in which much of the Great Basin was taken from them.

Jean Baptiste Charbonneau (Pomp, Pompy, Pompey) (1805–1866), son of Sacajawea and Toussaint Charbonneau, was born during the Lewis and Clark encampment among the Mandan people. During the journey to the Pacific Ocean and the return trip, Sacajawea carried the baby on her back. In St. Louis sometime after 1806, Meriwether Clark was asked to care for the boy. He eventually sent the child to a Catholic school.

Many years later, in 1823, Charbonneau was persuaded by Prince Paul Wilhelm of Germany to journey with him to Europe. He spent the next six years there, traveling and studying languages. Charbonneau returned to America with Prince Paul in 1829, and the two men explored the upper reaches of the Missouri River. Charbonneau became a fur trapper in an area of the Rocky Mountains that is now Utah and Idaho. He befriended several mountain men, including the legendary James Bridger, and joined in a trappers' rendezvous on the Green River in 1833.

When the fur trade declined in the 1830s, Charbonneau became a guide for explorers along the upper Missouri River. Along with Louis Vasquez and Andrew Sublette, he helped establish Fort Vasquez on the South Platte River near present-day Denver in 1839–1840. He explored the Yellowstone region with Scottish nobleman William Drummond in 1843. He also worked as a guide for the U.S. Corps of Topographical Engineers in 1845. A year later, during the Mexican War, he served as a guide for federal soldiers traveling from Santa Fe, New Mexico, to San Diego, California. After the war, he remained in California to prospect for gold. In 1866, while on his way to gold strikes in Montana, he died somewhere along the Owyhee River near the border of Oregon, Idaho, and Montana.

Pocatello (about 1815–1884), head chief of the Shoshone living in the Grouse Creek region, became leader in 1847—the same year that the Mormons arrived in Salt Lake City. As settlers and miners poured through the region, Native Americans made frequent raids for which Pocatello's band was often blamed. In later years, especially after he was briefly imprisoned in 1859, the great chief tried to maintain neutrality with the Mormons, miners, and other Native Americans in the region. In January 1863 he left Bear Hunter's village the day before the attack by Patrick E. Connor and his California volunteers. In July of that same year he negotiated with Governor James Doty and signed a peace treaty. From 1867 to 1869, he took part in buffalo hunts with Washakie's Wind River Shoshone and the Bannock.

In 1869, the Union Pacific and Central Pacific railroads joined at Promontory Point, Utah. With the completion of the transcontinental railroad, more settlers poured into the region. By the end of 1872,

Pocatello and his people, the Northwestern band of Shoshones, were forced to settle on the Fort Hall Reservation in southeastern Idaho. Pocatello converted to Mormonism to live at the farm of the missionary George Hill on the lower Bear River near Corrine, Utah. However, people in the town demanded that the converts, including Pocatello, be returned to the reservation. Rejecting Mormonism, Pocatello lived the rest of his life on the reservation. A nearby city in Idaho is named for him.

Sacajawea (Bird Woman) (about 1784–about 1812 or 1884), guide and interpreter for the Lewis and Clark expedition, was born among the Lemhi Shoshone who lived in what is now central Idaho and western Montana. When she was a teenager Sacajawea was taken captive by the Hidatsa and brought to their village on the upper Missouri River in present-day North Dakota. In 1804, she was either purchased or won in a wager by a French-Canadian trader named Toussaint Charbonneau. In May of that year, Lewis and Clark began their journey up the Missouri River from St. Louis. They wintered with the Mandan and met Charbonneau who they hired as an interpreter. The trader insisted that Sacajawea, who spoke Shoshone and who wished to rejoin her people, be allowed to travel with them.

In February of 1805—less than two months before the explorers left Fort Mandan in April—Sacajawea gave birth to Charbonneau's son, Jean Baptiste, who was nicknamed Pomp during the expedition. With a cradle-board on her back, Sacajawea played a major role in the success of the journey. She guided the explorers through the wilderness and helped sustain them with wild plants. Through sign language, she was able to communicate with all the native peoples encountered during the journey. She even served as a peacemaker with hostile Indians.

In August, at the Three Forks of the Missouri River in what is now Montana, she was finally reunited with her brother Cameahwait. At Sacajawea's request, Camaeahwait, who was now chief of his band, provided horses, supplies, and guides to help the expedition cross the Rocky Mountains. In November 1805, the expedition reached the Pacific Ocean.

Sacajawea

On the return trip, Sacajawea traveled with Clark's party along the Yellowstone River. She and Charbonneau left the expedition at the Hidatsa village on the Knife River while Lewis and Clark returned to St. Louis in 1806.

No one knows when or where Sacajawea died, and the accounts vary dramatically. In one version, she and Charbonneau came to St. Louis after 1806 and left their son with Clark to be educated. With trader Manuel Lisa, the couple then journeyed back up the Missouri River where Sacajawea died from an unknown disease in 1812. In another account, Sacajawea lived with the Comanches, then returned to her homeland and lived at Washakie's Wind River Reservation in Wyoming until her death at about 100 years of age.

Sacajawea has been honored in many history books and memorials, including a recently minted gold-colored coin. A river, mountain, and pass are also named for her.

Tendoy (Tendoi) (about 1834–1907), principal chief of the Lemhis, was born near the Boise River in Idaho. The son of a Bannock war chief and a Shoshone woman, Tendoy became the leader of a band of Bannock and Shoshone who made their home in the Lemhi Valley of Idaho. The band lived by fishing in the Lemhi and Salmon Rivers and buffalo hunting in western Montana. However, when gold prospectors flooded into the region in the 1860s, they so disrupted the traditional ways of hunting and gathering that Tendoy's people faced starvation.

Tendoy worked to maintain peaceful relations with the men in the Montana mining camps, as he made trading journeys to provide for his band. In 1868, the federal government established the Fort Hall Reservation in southeastern Idaho, but Tendoy and his people remained in the Lemhi Valley to the north. Like the Wind River Band of Eastern Shoshones under the leadership of Washakie, Tendoy remained peaceful through many conflicts in the region. These included raids by Pocatello and Bear Hunter in the 1850s and 1860s, the Paiute War of 1860, the Nez Perce War in 1877, and the Bannock War of 1878.

Tendoy

In 1875, President Ulysses S. Grant issued an executive order allowing Tendoy and his people to remain on their ancestral lands. However, in 1892 he was forced to sign a treaty with the government and finally settled on the Fort Hall Reservation. The editor of the *Idaho Recorder* newspaper of Salmon City wrote of the removal, "Now the crowning sorrow is forced upon this good chief and his long suffering band. They are being forced from the land of their birth, from the beautiful Lemhi valley, to a distant reservation to make homes among people whom they fear and dislike to the extreme of hate. The heart of the good Tendoy is broken by this last act of ingratitude." Tendoy's descendants live on the Fort Hall Reservation.

Washakie (Gourd Rattle) (about 1804–1900), principal chief of the Eastern Shoshone, spent his early years in the Bitterroot Mountains in what is now Montana with the Flathead tribe of his father. After his father's death, Washakie and his Shoshone mother went to live with her people in the Wind River Mountains, a range of the Rockies in what is now western Wyoming. As a young man, Washakie became renowned as a warrior in raids against the Blackfeet and Crow.

Like the Lemhi Shoshone under the leadership of Tendoy, the Wind River Shoshone (also known as the Eastern Shoshone), maintained peaceful relations with trappers and traders. During the 1820s and 1830s, Washakie became friends with Kit Carson, James Bridger, and other mountain men. Washakie hunted and trapped animals for pelts that he traded for guns, tools, and cloth. He also encouraged his people to trade furs for goods. By the late 1840s, Washakie had become the principal chief of his band. He remained friendly with the settlers making their way along the Oregon Trail and even ordered groups of warriors to patrol the region and help travelers to ford rivers and find lost livestock. He became friends with the Mormons and spent part of one winter in the home of their leader, Brigham Young.

During the campaign against Bear Hunter's band in January 1863, Washakie led his people to safety at Fort Bridger. In July 1863, he signed

Washakie

a treaty allowing settlers for twenty years to travel peacefully through his territory in exchange for payments. In July 1868, he signed another treaty granting a right-of-way to the Union Pacific Railroad and agreeing to settle on a reservation. After federal troops had established Camp Brown at what is now Lander, Wyoming, Washakie and other men in his band served as scouts in army campaigns against the Sioux, Cheyenne, Arapaho, and Ute.

In 1878, Camp Brown, which had been moved to the north and south forks of the Little Wind River, was renamed Fort Washakie. The same year—despite Washakie's protests—the Arapaho were moved to the Wind River Reservation with the Shoshone. In 1883, President Chester Arthur, who was on a fishing trip to Yellowstone National Park, visited Washakie. When his son died in a bar fight in 1897, Washakie converted to Christianity. He died three years later at Flathead Village in the Bitterroot Valley of Montana. He was buried in the Fort Washakie cemetery with full military honors.

Glossary

Appe Meaning "father," name given the sun, revered by the Western Shoshone as the creator of heaven and earth

Bannock a Northern Paiute group that moved from Oregon into Idaho and lived with the Northern Shoshone; Bannock people today share Fort Hall Reservation with the Shoshone

camas a kind of lily whose bulbs were dug and eaten by the Shoshone and other native peoples

counting coup touching an enemy in battle to prove one's bravery

Great Basin an arid region that includes Utah, Nevada, and parts of the adjoining states

Great Plains a vast area of flat or gently rolling grasslands between the Mississippi River and the Rocky Mountains

Louisiana Purchase a tract of land bought by the United States from France in 1803 comprising the territory west of the Mississippi River

moccasins soft leather shoes often decorated with brightly colored beads

Numic a branch of the Uto-Aztecan language family that includes Shoshone, Ute, and other languages of the Great Basin

parfleche a leather pouch for storing food, clothing, and other belongings

pemmican dried, pounded meat mixed with fat and berries, used as energy food by warriors on long journeys

piñon a small pine tree of the American Southwest that bears seeds collected and eaten by the Shoshone and other native people

pohakanti Shoshone medicine men

reservation a tract of land set aside for Native Americans

sweat lodge a dome-shaped hut of sticks covered with buffalo skins or mud in which purifications and other sacred ceremonies are held

taboo a strict prohibition, something that is forbidden

tipi a portable, cone-shaped home made of poles covered with animal skins

travois a sled made of two poles lashed together and pulled by a dog or horse

treaty a signed, legal agreement between two nations

Tribal Council the legal governing body for each Shoshone reservation

vision quest a ritual in which a person fasts and prays alone in hopes of receiving a vision from the spirits

weir   a trap placed across a stream or river to catch fish

Further Information

A number of excellent books about the Shoshone are available, including the following, several of which were consulted in the preparation of *The Shoshone*.

"The Origin of People" and "The Theft of Fire" are adapted from Western Shoshone stories collected by Julian H. Steward and published in *Some Western Shoshoni Myths*, Smithsonian Institution, Bureau of American Ethnology, Anthropological Papers, No. 31, 1943.

Clark, Ella E., and Margot Edmonds. *Sacagawea of the Lewis and Clark Expedition*. Berkeley: University of California Press, 1979.

Coolidge, Grace. *Teepee Neighbors*. Norman: University of Oklahoma Press, 1984.

Crum, Steven J. *The Road on Which We Came = Po'i Pentun Tammen Kimmappeh: A History of the Western Shoshone*. Salt Lake City: University of Utah Press, 1994.

Birchfield, D. L. *The Encyclopedia of North American Indians*. Tarrytown, NY: Marshall Cavendish, 1997.

Hebard, Grace Raymond. *Washakie: Chief of the Shoshones*. Lincoln: University of Nebraska Press, 1996.

Johansen, Bruce E., and Donald A. Grinde Jr. *The Encyclopedia of Native American Biography*. New York: Henry Holt and Co., 1997.

Langer, Howard J., ed. *American Indian Quotations*. Westport, CT: Greenwood Press, 1996.

Lohse, Ernest S., and Holmer, Richard N. *Fort Hall and the Shoshone-Bannock*. Pocatello, ID: Idaho State University Press, 1990.

Lowie, Robert Harry. *The Northern Shoshone*. New York: AMS Press, 1975.

Madsen, Brigham D. *The Lemhi: Sacajawea's People*. Caldwell, ID: Caxton Printers, 1979.

Malinowski, Sharon, and Anna Sheets. *The Gale Encyclopedia of Native American Tribes*. Detroit: Gale Research, 1998.

Malinowski, Sharon. *Notable Native Americans*. Detroit: Gale Research, 1995.

Murphy, Robert Francis, and Yolanda Murphy. *Shoshone-Bannock Subsistence and Society*. Berkeley: University of California Press, 1960.

O'Gara, Geoffrey. *What You See in Clear Water: Life on the Wind River Reservation*. New York: Alfred Knopf, 2000.

Paterek, Josephine. *Encyclopedia of American Indian Costume*. Santa Barbara, CA: ABC-CLIO, 1994.

Pritzker, Barry M. *Native Americans: An Encyclopedia of History, Culture, and Peoples*. Santa Barbara, CA: ABC-CLIO, 1998.

Smith, Anne M. *Shoshone Tales*. Salt Lake City: University of Utah Press, 1993.

Stamm, Henry E. *People of the Wind River: The Eastern Shoshones, 1825–1900*. Norman: University of Oklahoma Press, 1999.

Sturtevant, William C., and Warren L. D'Azevedo. *Handbook of North American Indians*. Volume 11. Great Basin. Washington, D.C.: Smithsonian Institution, 1986.

Trenholm, Virginia Cole. *The Shoshonis, Sentinels of the Rockies*. Norman: University of Oklahoma Press, 1981.

Vander, Judith. *Shoshone Ghost Dance Religion: Poetry Songs and Great Basin Context*. Urbana: University of Illinois Press, 1997.

Voget, Fred W. *The Shoshoni-Crow Sun Dance*. Norman: University of Oklahoma Press, 1984.

Wilson, Elijah Nicholas. *Among the Shoshones*. Salt Lake City: Skelton Publishing Co., 1910.

Children's Books

Burt, Olive Woolley. *Sacajawea*. New York: Franklin Watts, 1978.

Carter, Alden R. *The Shoshonis*. New York: Franklin Watts, 1989.

Dramer, Kim. *The Shoshone*. Philadelphia: Chelsea House, 1997.

Fradin, Dennis B. *Sacagawea: The Journey to the West*. Parsippany, NJ: Silver Press, 1998.

Gregory, Kristiana. *The Legend of Jimmy Spoon*. New York: Scholastic, 1990.

Heady, Eleanor B. *Sage Smoke: Tales of the Shoshoni-Bannock Indians*. Morristown, NJ: Silver Burdett Press, 1993.

Moss, Nathaniel. *The Shoshone Indians*. Broomall, PA: Chelsea Juniors, 1997.

Raphael, Elaine. *Sacajawea: The Journey West*. New York: Scholastic, 1994.

Roop, Peter *Girl of the Shining Mountains: Sacagawea's Story*. New York: Hyperion Books for Children, 1999.

Rowland, Della. *The Story of Sacajawea, Guide to Lewis and Clark*. Boston: Houghton Mifflin, 1997.

Sanford, William R. *Sacagawea: Native American Hero*. Springfield, NJ: Enslow Publishers, 1997.

Seymour, Flora Warren. *Sacagawea, American Pathfinder*. New York: Aladdin Books, 1991.

St. George, Judith. *Sacagawea*. New York: Putnam, 1997.

Stevens, Janet. *Old Bag of Bones: A Coyote Tale*. New York: Holiday House, 1996.

Thomasma, Kenneth. *The Truth about Sacajawea*. Jackson, WY: Grandview, 1997.

White, Alana. *Sacagawea: Westward with Lewis and Clark*. Springfield, NJ: Enslow, 1997.

Organizations

Battle Mountain Shoshone
35 Mountain View Drive, #138-13
Battle Mountain, NV 89820
Phone: 702-635-2004
Fax: 702-635-8016

Duckwater Shoshone
P.O. Box 140068
Duckwater, NV 89314
Phone: 702-863-0227
Fax: 702-863-0301

Elko Shoshone
P.O. Box 748
Elko, NV 89801
Phone: 702-738-8889
Fax: 702-753-5439

Ely Shoshone
16 Shoshone Circle
Ely, NV 89301
Phone: 702-289-3013
Fax: 702-289-3156

Fort McDermitt Shoshone-Paiute
P.O. Box 457
McDermitt, NV 89421
Phone: 702-532-8259
Fax: 702-532-8913

Fort Hall Bannock and Shoshone
P.O. Box 306
Fort Hall, ID 83203-0306
Phone: 208-238-3700
Fax: 208-237-0797

Northwestern Band of Shoshone
P.O. Box 637
Blackfoot, ID 83221
Phone: 208-785-7401
Fax: 208-785-2206

Shoshone of Wyoming
P.O. Box 217
Fort Washakie, WY 82514
Phone: 307-33-3532
Fax: 307-332-3055

Shoshone-Piaute
P.O. Box 219
Owyhee, NV 89832
Phone: 702-757-3161
Fax: 702-757-2219

South Park Shoshone
P.O. Box B-13
Lee, NV 89829
Phone: 702-744-4273

Te-Moak Shoshone
525 Sunset Street
Elko, NV 89801
Phone: 702-738-9251
Fax: 702-738-2345

Timba-Sha (Timbisha) Western Shoshone
(Death Valley Indian Community)
P.O. Box 206
Death Valley, CA 92328
Phone: 760-786-2374
Fax: 760- 786-2376

Wells Shoshone
P.O. Box 809
Wells, NV 89835
Phone: 702-752-3045

Yomba Shoshone
P.O. Box 6275
Austin, NV 89310
Phone: 702-964-2463
Fax: 702-964-2443

Websites

Several of these websites for the Shoshone organizations were consulted for this book.

Fallon Paiute-Shoshone Tribe
http://www.fpst.org/

Northern Utah Shoshone History
http://users.efortress.com/genealogy/page1.htm

Shoshone Bannock Tribal Enterprises
http://www.sho-ban.com/index.htm

Shoshone Business Council
http://tlc.wtp.net/shoshone.htm

Sosoni' daigwapeha Wihindeboope (Shoshoni Language Home Page)
http://www.isu.edu/departments/anthro/shoshoni/index.html

Western Shoshone Defense Project
http://www.alphacdc.com/wsdp/

Wind River Reservation (Eastern Shoshone & Northern Arapaho Tribes)
http://www.mnisose.org/25.html

Index

Page numbers in **boldface** are illustrations

Raymond Bial

HAS PUBLISHED MORE THAN THIRTY CRITICALLY ACCLAIMED BOOKS OF PHO-tographs for children and adults. His photo-essays for children include *Corn Belt Harvest*, *Amish Home*, *Frontier Home*, *Shaker Home*, *The Underground Railroad*, *Portrait of a Farm Family*, *With Needle and Thread: A Book About Quilts*, *Mist Over the Mountains: Appalachia and Its People*, *Cajun Home*, and *Where Lincoln Walked*.

He is currently immersed in writing *Lifeways*, a series of books about Native Americans. As with his other work, Bial's deep feeling for his subjects is evident in both the text and illustrations. He travels to tribal cultural centers, photographing homes, artifacts, and sur-roundings and learning firsthand about the national lifeways of these peoples.

A librarian at a small college in Champaign, Illinois, he lives with his wife and three children in nearby Urbana.